C000147696

Foothold

Pam Zinnemann-Hope

Ward Wood Publishing
www.wardwoodpublishing.co.uk

Published by Ward Wood Publishing
6 The Drive
Golders Green
London NW11 9SR
www.wardwoodpublishing.co.uk

The right of Pam Zinnemann-Hope to be identified as author of this work has been asserted by her in accordance with the Copyright, Designs and Patent Act, 1988.

Copyright © 2017 Pam Zinnemann-Hope
ISBN: 978-1-908742-65-0

British Library Cataloguing in Publication Data. A CIP record for this book can be obtained from the British Library.

All rights reserved. No part of this publication may be reproduced, stored in a retrieval system, or transmitted in any form or by any means, electronic, mechanical, photocopying, recording or otherwise without the prior written permission of the publishers. This book may not be lent, hired out, resold or otherwise disposed of by way of trade in any form of binding or cover other than that in which it is published, without the prior consent of the publishers.

Designed and typeset in Palatino Linotype by Ward Wood Publishing.
Cover design by Ward Wood Publishing.
Cover image:
'The Bishop's Curl' linocut by Liz Somerville
www.lizsomerville.co.uk

Printed and bound in Great Britain by
Imprint Digital, Seychelles Farm,
Upton Pyne, Exeter, Devon EX5 5HY

For Peter, For Henry

Contents

Foothold

In A Museum
by Thomas Hardy

1

Here's the mould of a musical bird long passed from light,
Which over the earth before man came was winging;
There's a contralto voice I heard last night,
That lodges with me still in its sweet singing.

II

Such a dream is Time that the coo of this ancient bird
Has perished not, but is blent, or will be blending
Mid visionless wilds of space with the voice that I heard,
In the full-fugued song of the universe unending.

They Tell Us It Will Come Tonight

There's a sense of waiting
for when life's contracted to our valley:
every shape described by white.

Let it bring that certain hush
to the river's rage and roar
leaving the climate in parenthesis,

let it lie, firm and crunchy in the morning
crystalline yet soft-appearing
sun shining till it dazzles:

let us feel intrepid then
unafraid to walk out, or toboggan,
because our bones are brittled.

Remember when Henry was newborn,
blue eyes entranced one morning
by the wide world of my dressing gown,

its white fields, his first snow.

Night Song

Through the dark come the sounds
of your strong, short breaths,
your out-breaths and silent ins,
as you lie sleeping.
Lying beside you, with my love
– long-lived – revived again
I can feel your pulse slow-beating.

Now you've curled around me,
this habit of ours. And it's quiet:
the screech owl's stopped
his intimate screeching just outside
our window, ceased repeating his calling
over the water meadow's ancient ridges,
its reedy furrows silted from flooding.

I picture the meadow's daylight colours
that shift like our passions:
frost bitten grass, through flag-iris gold
and electric green that softens,
as you lie here, probably dreaming.
When we met your longer legs
strode ahead, you never ambled.

Now time has slowed your pace
against mine. Count
one stride to a decade,
unstoppable walking; you're always
one and a half great strides ahead

my long lived love.

Through

Through the window
I watch the half-moon
rise from behind
a crowd of bare trees
quietly waving
their arms in the dark

Mary Anning To Her Father

Let them point at me, with their taffety fingers.

Must figure how these bones fit, Pa,
by lamplight, against incoming tide.

Never mind toes numb of cold,
I'm obsessed, like you, in your days.
Can't stay in after storm.

'*Ichthyosaurus communis*'
been my latest find.

His eye sockets gawked at me
in my workshop back at home

where daily I dream my woman's name
might live on and on,
till sea come in and wash us
all to extinction.

Some days there be scaly skin;
inside one crittur's ribs, fish he eaten.

Hark now! Clatter of rocks.
Must wait here for its ceasing.

> You, Pa, in Heaven, you
> be the one who first taught me!

Look at these bones:
snake-like neck, turtle-shaped head.
I'm handling him – first.

December's Reckoning

This afternoon is still.
My eyes fetch the grey across
the field's frost-scorched grass.

A rook's cruck-cruck sees off
a flock of sparrows from the silent trees;
silhouettes of flitting arrow-heads.

I walk here with my scattered dreams;
the unmade and the gone-wrong.

I need to sing out
the wasting year...

Gurk! Gurk!
Is it a winter frog?
Or a water bird?

...Nothing to be seen down there,
no movement from behind the browned hedge.

Does it sense, the creature from the stream,
how soon the light will begin returning?

Distances i

Focus

From the house I step
across the gravel, the grass:

the distance between us.
There is this pull

to your studio,
to where I know

you bend to work,
eyes focused

on the black notes
you place on the staves

in a world of sound
I cannot enter.

Threshold

'The night in its fullness met her flatly on the threshold, like the very brink of an absolute void, or the ante-mundane Ginnungs-Gap believed in by her Teuton forefathers. For her eyes were fresh from the blaze, & here there was no street lamp or lantern to form a kindly transition between inner glare and outer dark.'

Thomas Hardy, *The Woodlanders*

There are no street lights. It's late December and I'm standing here, by the window, facing east. There's been no sun all afternoon.

Just now that line of big trees by the riverbank is becoming clearer, so that I can see every twig, and even, in the treetops, the nodes on the twigs – beech, sycamore, ash. Where branches overlap they form nests: around several nests, gaps of grey light.

Now the twigs are blurring and the silhouettes of the large limbs are blackening; every curve becomes clear, becomes velvet, almost purple. The grey of the sky turns slightly bluer: a violet tone begins.

The nests are smudgier now; paler smudges in between. Even the dark limbs loosen a little, even their colour. They are slowly withdrawing from me, becoming other; saddening me now, in this heavy half-light.

The trees are growing taller. All but the nearest have moved closer together and the one flings out his limbs in a flamboyant gesture of defiance.

Now they are going down, slowly, into the dark. One is spreading himself and telling a story and becoming a squirrel, a giant Ratatoskr, the messenger in the world tree, as he goes. The taller ones stretch out their arms to protect the smaller.

They are shrinking now: no nests; no limbs, except for the nearest; and his are shrivelling. I'm barely aware of trunks and crowns; the squirrel, the messenger, still holding forth, baffled. The furthest tree a blur of indigo-black, the nearest still flings his thin limbs.

The small light from inside the room, here, is reflecting on the window, it's becoming harder to see. The nearest tree is gone now. Ratatoskr is lost. The blackness is inscrutable.

Distances ii

Listen

I think this piece is almost finished.
You look at me.
                    Will you listen?

Now I'm in the old feeding chair
with the tree of life cushion:

I'm watching you stand:
                    you like to stand;

by the white wall
                    you slot in the CD you've
                    burned on your computer.

A bassoon trills,

                    the first notes hold us,

                    carry us...

Small Nettles

'Tall nettles cover up...'

Dear Edward Thomas,

Small nettles nestle in iced lane-side mud
with dock, plantain, strawberry, celandine:
tender leaves below the hedge, hoar-frosted,
this rare cold day in a winter of rain.
And you come to mind.

A January with grass so green was never known:
all the records say we've had the warmest year,
though frozen tyre prints striped with shadows
mark a moment when two cars passed here.

Dorset,
January, 2016

Eurydice

First, one, a white flame,
lighting my way; it beckons
from the top of the steep path

as I follow Orpheus
in my slow, dazed climb;
I keep on shambling behind him.

Next, white tepals gradually spreading,
snowdrops flock in the distance,
among the trees and in the hedgerows.

Their music seems to have sprung
out of my dream of winter,
from deep in my shawl of earth.

I hear the harmony, faintly.
Orpheus plays counterpoint on his lyre.
Listen! he cries.

And spins to face me.
I turn back, to my bed of earth.
Snowdrops chant in my place.

Naming Scelidosaurus

When the lid of time rolls back...

'Now' is an island in a tropical lagoon;
a herd of horned creatures meanders
among conifers, tree ferns, cycads;
there's no-one to name them; there are no words;
it's *In the beginning...*

They have their bonds, intimacies of family.
One eye on the young, in the pouring rain,
their sharp teeth busy slicing the foliage,
somehow, they miss the hiss, or rumble,
from the distant quake.

The great wave comes, there's nowhere to run,
they're washed up, then sucked down
into a sea where they sink into sand,
oxygen starved; where the calcite forms.
It's *In the end*

And *In the beginning* and *In the end*
they're bedded in rock, where they wait;
geographies come; geographies go,
rocks fall, and rise up,
the herd of creatures still lost to view...

Till a man looks down, to the ground at his feet.
And, as with Adam and the beasts in his story,
a human voice must find them a name
from a jigsaw of their island lives,
and bones, slipped under the lid of time.

Central Heating

How scraps of straw under floorboards upstairs
were relics of thatch from before the slates,
how our floorboards themselves, thin as paper,
began to crumble in his hands
as he lifted them to lay piping.
'It's like Gladwell's roof,
over to Cattistock,'
how he intoned it, remember:

'I went up there to the loft
wanting to site the water tank.
No felting; leaks; beams worm-eaten;
joists rotten. Like now,
the middle of winter, bitter;
roofers all busy, men that came
not my first choice, or my second.
Your new floorboards,
bedroom, landing, study,
could hold you up two weeks, a month.'

Employing Tom, our local plumber
– how that became an act of faith!
He had an incantation
for every room he plumbed;
in his known geography of hereabouts
each corner was recalled by a story
of a chimney fire,
two dead bats in a water tank,
a narrow escape from flooding;
his memory a vast diagram of challenges
continually re-configured. Remember

how on the table, as he spoke,
our star gazers' white petals flushed
deep pink, with wine-dark stipples,
in the glass vase; the green buds
lifted their pointed tips to heaven
like a prayer to ancient gods for us
– uncertain what else he might find –
that's how we started out here together,
knowing no-one, new to this place.

March Notes

Deep yellow lives
            humming
along the field's edges
            catkins swarming around hazels.

         *

A hailstorm
            willow branches
where light falls
            raindrops in budburst.

'No-one's died, it can't be that dire'

The earth's axis tilts towards the sun,
it's spring: sudden and surprising, the way
the season fizzes with light, each day
different still, after sixty-seven seed times.
You tell me about her, her marriage is
dissolving, her heart's being ratcheted down.

I'm in the kitchen with the phone to my ear
staring out at the sky to the hill over there,
and greens of fresh foliage all
interlaced, suddenly skewing the view
 – where the wide and thin trunks stand in a line,
until next year now the hill's disappearing.

We can't save her from disillusion.
My eyes search along the stone garden path
to the field beyond: tight hawthorn buds
on fresh stems, maroons and deep reds.
Somewhere a planet shifts in its orbit;
and for a moment everything stops.

You, House Martins

Welcome back, after your long-haul flight
as you dive and weave on forget-me-not sky.
Remember, please, generations who came before;
this house was their nesting place.
Come back! Come back to my house.

Build a home of mud from the river,
daub five or six more on the weather boards
and one above the back door – where, years ago,
young peeped out, twitter-babbling;
as I passed I 'hello-ed' up to them.

Was it the last cat, killing the young
in their maiden flight? Was it the sparrows
shoving the parents out? Forget all that.
Were some of your forebears lost over Africa?
Come back, in the light of this sudden, burning sun.

Hooke Woods, In Two Movements

For my small grandson, Henry

It's snowing beech husks thick and fast,
and leaves slowly shake their liquid green
out of soft brown husks.
It's silent here. But not quite silent:
a wren's call tsipps, like a tiny silver axe.
And an old memory lifts me towards
a high roof, sandstone vaulting: a dream
meant to erase the memories of all dark ages.
The wind's tuning up. It shooshes and hushes
as though we could enter or leave
this spring, any time of year.

You take your small, fast steps
among long purple pools of bluebells
striped with sun: among their vast scent,
along boggy paths, leaf-littered russet
and beige; this experience, of being a child
in bluebell woods, is handed down to us:
in this moment you
discover live and dead dung beetles,
small spiders spinning webs on sedge;
you balance on stray log bridges;
it's not yet in your gift to understand
there's an inscription here, held in each tree:
history in rings and in the pattern of its branchings,
it tells of drought, storms, insect attacks: circumstance.

3 Liszt Études
i.m. Molly

La Leggierezza

the first few notes
play around

seem to roll a ball
seem to recall

that way of bowling along
that way of the dog

Transcendental Étude

o small brown dog almost black
you do not you run across a unified field

you trot at my heel
while i read about string theory

you with your studded leather collar
you walk on and sniff

verges and hedgerows
with your soft wet nose

question air and landscape
read badger fox rat mouse

while i search and search

what is death where do we go
where do we come from
why don't we know

you know dinner time
your little routines

i read that space-time is curved
you run across the curve of the cut green field

you search for sticks
discover how to fit two sticks in the mouth

Il Lamento, or Instructions
for Juggling a Three-Foot Stick

the tenderest of dances
a clustering of notes...

playful dark

juggling juggling

snout under stick
butt it butt it
up it goes

a little way

into the air

catch it on snout

balance balance it
slight nod
slight lift of head

toss it
catch it

wriggle juggle
till it drops

snout under it
begin again

the melody comes into its own
improvising

Crab Apple

As if a many-armed god waving at me
could summon my faith in renewal;
as if his greeting could bulge out
the tight buds on his arms till they spill
into palest pink, almost white, when he comes
into leaf, there, by the path in the garden;
as if my heart lifts and while the blackbird
calls his refrain – semi-quaver, quaver, glissando –
I could believe our garden might live forever
in this one day under clearest azure;
let's believe it now, and forget how this
is the time of year the rest of the year
works up to, and down from: a brief god,
waving to us, with a blackbird on his shoulder.

The Musicologist And The Birdwatcher

I can't help thinking of them
every time I hear the lark.
Every time I hear the lark,
I think of them,
as I walk around the rim of Eggardon.

It sings above the outer ramparts,
it sings above the grassy top
of the hill fort as I walk back;
sometimes I see it, rising above me,
a dark dot, trilling its grace notes.

Every time, like today,
I remember a programme,
the one with the two men walking,
the camera panning the blue above them,
its focus on the singing bird:

how when they get home, they slow
the recording they've made;
they slow it; they play it backwards.
Quickly the musicologist annotates.
Now he plays six bars of Beethoven.

Identical, he says,
the camera panning the score.
*Oh! The obsessive musicality
of the bird brain*! says the ornithologist.
They marvel at the attentiveness of Beethoven.

If I had my way I'd make a sequel,
I'd make a sequel
about how Beethoven's soul
has entered the lark, backwards;
how it's speeded up.

June Notes

Early morning steam
rises from the pink grasses;

by the house wall
a rose-slugworm

is spoiling the roses
infinitesimally   slowly.

                    *

Birdsong and the shooshing
of the mill race:

I'm crossing the wide lawn,
knife in hand, to cut fresh lettuce.

                    *

There, look! On the path!
Red crest,

yellow bird-back.
Woodpecker.

Yaffle-yaffling
he flies off.

                    *

The neighbours' mower
buzzes, buzzes;

a bee visits
clematis jackmanii,

azure campanulas
silently.

*

Night-time:

rubbish in hand
I head for the bin,

find a tiny, green
fluorescent light;

bend to her stone slab,
hold my first glow-worm.

Listening To Liszt

Notes ripple like a river,
a CD is playing *Un Sospiro*.

I watch you sink slowly into a low chair
you groan like the strained hinges of the door.

I catch myself thinking,
Soon he'll be back to normal.

Complex textures rise and fall;
through open French windows, warmth

insinuates between thin white curtains
that veil the square:

I'm seeing the younger you,
soft, blond skin, thick, long curls;

lithe and quick, the one
who travels with me always,

the one I'm waiting for when I wait
for you. He's one of many.

Which one is he? Light
that teases from your eyes,

wicked words that flicker on your tongue?
An arpeggio descends like a small waterfall.

Each one of you, inside the other, down the years,
nests, like a *matryoshka*, inside my heart.

The music is a single breath
Un Sospiro

The Stone Balancer's Secret

For Adrian Gray

I can't stop dreaming
of the life of stones

their pitch and poise
angles that
tangle my mind.

No blue tack
no glue no velcro.

No tricks?

Only the trick
that gravity pulls.

Look!

I brace my back
raise a huge rock
to vertical

heft a top stone up
and slowly drop
its tapered point

– right hand stays above
left below –

like lifting baby
into the bath –

onto the neck
of the base rock.

I listen
through my fingertips:

earth's crust's
bulge and crush

sea's crash
and wash

hear the exact point
of friction:

stone balances
on the other's neck

a head cocked
to one side;

I cradle stone's birth
and stone's death

for that moment I'm a god
making a person.

Stone draws breath
I step back.

Stone pulls its weight
a displacement of air

in stasis
stone flies.

Back Door

Come quick, said the cat, at 5.40 am.
Thinking him hungry I went downstairs

into the light,
to find back door

and front windows
wide open

after yesterday's great heat,
the whole house cool and fresh,

the garden still as the pause
between in and out breath

in the early midsummer's
soft radiance

as though it were not
my forgetfulness the cat was leading me to

but locks and handles with a secret life,
a house's transfiguration

until I thought to check
where my handbag was.

Of Blue Water

Lulworth

In the deep circle of water
with the anchored boats bobbing
on the blue surface, where, above it,
the cliff face folds in a crumple
of layers thrust up, a fold in time,
and two people walk along the cliff path,
chalky earth trodden hard in the long heat:
here, in the late afternoon sun
a mother and her small daughter take
a dip together; out of the blue
two fishermen roll a boat up a long plank
onto the sun-dusted beach
where I sit quietly on a rock;

the clanking boat on the rollers,
the daughter crying out
at the chill of the sudden water,
the walkers dripping sweat,
the cliffs holding and letting go
the slight weight
of their footsteps,
the sea flopping its edges
against the rock
stand and move in the mind's eye
this morning, the moment
before waking

When Brendel Appears At Plush

Out of the dark, suddenly spotlit by the car,
still in the black suit he wore for his performance,
he's walking as though this were his habitual walk
towards a door he's always about to enter;
grey curls almost touching his collar,
he cradles the black folio under his arm
with the practice of one
who feels the measure of every note
and weighs each pause;

and though it's summer and dry, and his mind and body,
in spite of a little stiffness in the back,
are still finely attuned to the music
he's just been playing, and he knows how to make
the piano sing like a human voice,
here's a man who, blindfold,
could find his way through the landscape
by the sounds of the rain on its surfaces.

Brim

So summer sings its song
and honeysuckle puffs its honey scent

in the dead of night the river hums
a sensor light comes on

beside tall flowers a fox sits still
now panicky he runs

a ginger cat from behind a tree
sprints after him across the lawn.

In the warmth of day the air smells green
and tiny apples slowly swell

a bee sips from a nectar cup
still summer sings its song.

More leaves than stars in the milky way
the lawn's a sky of clover

how can we know the lives of plants
when the silent sap brims over?

Distances iii

Mobile

I'm coasting along in neutral
– that peculiar emotional gear –
travelling away from you today,
on the train to London;

I'm carrying your desire
to talk to me tonight
in my pocket, squeezed
beside my mobile.

I'm wondering
how I can fit you in,
between dinner
and this evening's *Russian Translations*.

Tonight I'll be seeing my friends.
And you'll be at home
with the piano and the cat.

Visiting Norrie

i.m. Norrie Woodhall

This woman, whose sister once played Tess
when she played Liza-Lu for Thomas Hardy,

slowly, with an aid, ferries me through
her house that floats in a liquid light
filtered through garden trees;

and does she almost live
her own myth (alone, here now),
while her papers and books shift bravely around?

And does she ever recite his
'Who's In The Next Room?'
while the furniture holds fast to its place?

We have no recording of Hardy
but I hear his voice in my head.

How did Hardy speak?
With a Dorset accent? I ask.

        Oh no! He'd been to London.

And his voice?
Was it high? Or low?

Through labyrinths of fading synapses
a hundred and five years old,
Norrie consults her girlish self:

Medium, I'd say. And he was soft
spoken. A shy man. You could tell.

Something flits between us,
neither heard nor spoken,
her velvet curtains drawn against the sun.

About Exile

Where before there was an openness,
suddenly her brown eyes are impenetrable.
She talks about her own country;
the hot dusty place where she where she began her life,
fresh pomegranates, the harbour;
when she touches on the living texture of marble and bees,
I see the shutters go up at the windows of her old house.

And I know the stone her clear song springs from.

Sky Blue

From a residency reading poetry to patients on the elderly care
wards in Dorset County Hospital

The raised bed rail anchored him, as he turned
towards me in his sky blue pyjamas.
Perhaps it was the shock of his recent stroke
that brightened those cobalt eyes looking out.
And when he told me he was fond of Wordsworth,
and then of his own namesake, I pulled out
my Complete Robert Frost.

He said, *I don't read novels. Only poems.*
And facts. But I'm too tired to read
for myself now. Thank you for doing it.
And as I read he seemed to be working
something out, a kind of going over
his life, checking that it was good enough
and weighed right.

After this first day on the ward I walked out
into the hot summer evening and drove
to Eggardon Hill, for a view of the sea.
I began climbing, fast, until I stood
on the edge of ancient earth ramparts,
the deep drop to the thicket where deer hide.

When I gazed to west and south, towards
the whole expanse of sea in Lyme Bay
it was covered, as though it had never existed,
by white cloud that stopped
at the coast-line exactly; as though
this island and this life had been raised
above the earth, into some cloud country.

The next week, when I saw Mr Frost,
a dullness began entering his eyes,
and he told me,
I dreamt of apple picking in your garden.

Perseids

That night we all stood on the rim of our dreams,
the summer before your first child was born,
the summer my youngest was leaving home;

the night the two of you lay on your backs
in the lane, on your coats, it was the peak
of the Perseids

– and you lay under a clear sky,
sprinkled with the pinhead lights of stars,
they were switched on and dancing,

over water meadows and bog alders,
millions of light years away –
the two of you stayed quiet in the lane.

Then, *Wh e e e e e e!*
I came and joined you for the next one;
rocket-like – as though you could hear

its hiss – till it cut out.
Each few seconds a meteor
ran the sky, as we whooped,

kicked our legs in the air as it fell;
tiny, invisible bits of dust and rock;
meteoroid, briefly becoming a hair-thin

fire trail, if we could catch it.
They kept on coming, each
as if with a perfect aim,

randomly, hundreds of thousands of miles,
before we could blink.
And whatever our aims at that time,
we fell to magical thinking,
felt a need for a light to keep
in a pocket, like in the song;

while 'stars' were falling through the night
burning as they hit our earth's atmosphere

dust to the planet's mass.

Visit

Hardy's Cottage 'Here is the ancient floor…'

I came here once before,
hoping to cheer my mother,
I walked up the lane with her
on her last visit to me.

We stepped through the garden gate
on a fresh summer's afternoon.
Though often far apart,
we connected, in sudden delight.

The lupins were salmon and mauve;
I remember her pleasure in trees
– something living and older than her;
the delphiniums, the colours of words.

In Our Beginning

For Peter

The ticket inspector comes round
to check our tickets to Waterloo;
we're dressed for a pre-Christmas wedding,
you in your suit with the purple stripes,
your best coat and broad-brimmed hat,
I, in my fake fur, jewellery all a-glitter,
and he doesn't bother to ask
for our senior citizen's railcards.

We could be cheating, I say to you
after he's gone, even at our age!
Think of that eighty-year-old man
who murdered a ninety-year-old woman
in a care home, last week,
maybe because of dementia,
which can manifest violence in some,
probably a peace-loving man,

until a while before that moment when...

Who knows what you and I might still become?
Let's think of all our becomings:
separate dreams and fears
to knowing one another – heart,
blood, beautiful skin, its warts an' all;
separate pasts with their own unfoldings
to last summer's garden full of children –
our children's children in a water fight...

I can see you now, in your nineties,
music played as much as Elliott Carter's
but with tunes;
me, my writing read as much as Mary Wesley's;

and with children's children's children,
we're sitting in some clichéd, hazy sunset, till
blindness, deafness, What did you say?
the Zimmer, the little shopping trolley,
paralysis – whatever slowly befalls us;
and if we're lucky, simply before the drop-dead-
gorgeously-quick last movement, last breath,
the last great cadenza…

A Particular Bee

In the sun's heat a distant fowl calls,
tick and broom of a passing van,
coo coo roo coo of wood pigeon in tree.

In the garden a particular bee dances
an angular dance around pale purple phlox,
wing-shifts upwards, to white honeysuckle,
it tries, tries again, fails to find.

Then, hover and move, hover and move
to edge of phlox, to purple woundwort
that wafts in spires. Bee tries
a tiny tired flower mouth, another.
Retreats. Rises
to large, fresh woundwort flower:
at last plunges
into nectar, headfirst.

Cave

I entered a deep cave
in a sandstone cliff;

bowed my head
where the roof was low;

huddled in the centre
of a narrow passage

with its twists and turns
of rough, bare rock.

I learned
of the palettes found,

and the crayon sticks;
the iron oxide, ground:

pigment, mixed with water,
juices, urine, blood;

how it was poured
into hollow bones,

the reds, ochres, browns
and charcoal black,

to be air-brushed
onto the rock.

So as not to destroy
the images from the past

the guide lit them, briefly,
with her infrared light.

There was once a flickering,
tallow torch. It burned

the precious animal fats.
Someone held it for *him*:

a man who painted a bison,
the bison that follows you

with its eyes, as you move;
and he spoke to me,

across fifteen millenia,
with a gesture of the hand,

'Hello. Look, here!'
It's in the rock, a vision,

bulked out of the contours
and shaded.

And I'm here, trying
to paint pictures with words,

using black ink on paper.
By the time you have these

they'll be figured on a screen,
and printed:

this conversation with someone
who painted animals

in mined haematite;
haema, meaning blood.

Distances iv

Return, Like Love

I've drunk not quite hot enough tea
just short of the mark in the cup
and I've eaten a pastry
pronounced like a hurt
by the girl who served it
on the train:
'pain' au chocolat.

Blown Loose

Jade and sulphur-yellow
hover, by my office window.

It's a brimstone. I watched one
in the garden last week

vie for nectar with cabbage whites
then alight on purple loosestrife.

It had the veined and luminous undersides,
the large, orange-brown spots in the butterfly book;

it unfolded its wings
with the flare of late summer's passions.

This one now, has the flight of a brimstone
but it's falling.

It's a leaf blown loose from the hornbeam;
autumn has shifted the light.

To The Little Egret

Between two garden sheds
I glance through to the river

sudden sun lights the white
silent lift of wingspan

I continue my work
miss your quicksilver catch.

A Walk Before Rain With Henry

In a split-second it flits, close as a kiss.
Darts around an invisible, hairpin bend.

In the blink of an eye a dark shape
veers up over the high hedge.

It almost scared you?

Another skims past
in the dusky lane.

We turn. It's gone, this alien creature,
silent, let loose by low, dark cloud.

One swoops in, at eye level.
Double loops. – Bats?

Pipistrelles and Brandt's,
they roosted here once,

are they returning?
Too early in the evening!

A flash of white on the underside.
Oh! A forked tail, barely visible.

Henry, they're swallows!
– Belong to the day, like us
but feather and skin.

One comes in from behind, at ankle level.
It's charting the course of the lane.

Like a spaceship in Star Wars.
It's hunting its supper.

It arcs and whizzes,
aerobatics that shape the summer.

Sky lightens.
No rain.
They're gone.

One Thing Leads

Going to the orchard, black sack in hand
to rake up the walnut leaves and bag them,
is not exactly a direct route to work,
especially when it involves finding
and hulling walnuts in rubber gloves.
And however much I hurry, one thing leads
to another: I become dizzy from crouching
to pick up leaves, then straightening; lean the rake
on the tree, bemoan my ageing body,
and lose my thread;
take the nuts indoors to the sink and begin
scraping the thread-like fibres
where the green pods were attached
with a sharp knife.
                    Walnut hunting is fun,
it's like Easter egg hunting in autumn,
but why do I bother when this year
the shells are too soft? And I'm late,
now, starting my work and don't know
where to begin. I need to wash the dog's bedding
make phone calls, worm the cat
before my grandson comes, do some cleaning.
I need to crack on with something…

Autumn Song

dear leaf
dear life
lift up
fly by

fly by
dear life
dear leaf
lift up

lift up
fly by
dear leaf
dear life

Scavengers

Eype

Hunting for scarce treasure
– five-tentacled Jurassic scavenger –
what are we hoping for
in filigreed stone,
fallen from the cliff?
If we could roll back
from the modern creature,
beyond human sound;

our time smaller
than a dot on an i in one hundred
and ninety-five million, the years
beyond mind's stretch and sea's reach,
beyond bodies imprinted in stone…

– Impossible journey! –

The incoming tide turns us back
till we spy an endless ribbon,
shining above the shore line:

tiny, iridescent bodies, whitebait;
chased in by a shoal of mackerel,
they've leapt out of the mouth
of one death, to this.

We gather the freshest in Jane's kagool,
carry them home; wash, flour
and shallow fry them; dry them
with paper, pepper them with parsley,

we feel the crispy salt water flavour
explode in our mouths. Jane says,
I wonder how brittle star tasted.

A Certain Morning

What becomes you most?
Becoming: or unbecoming?
Continually flowing in
a rearranging of each other.

Take the morning music off the hook,
let the morning come and look
at you and me, and what is
to come or not; we're each,
moving, uncertain
in a certain changing morning.

Young Silver Birches
After the Storm

One lies on the ground,
two naked limbs
reaching up.

Another has fallen
into the embrace
of its neighbour.

Of the remaining
many have snapped,
stand headless.

Some of these
still carry leaves; green,
through beige, to brown,

they brush
against trunks
that gleam like skin

You're Almost Facing Me

Here in the curtained cubicle you
undress for the doctor and the nurse
to check your skin for minor cancers.
I sit watching you from the distance
Lucien Freud stands from the viewer
in 'Painter Working, Reflection'.
He's naked, except for his undone shoes,
palette knife in hand. It would be
a half-written music score if it were you.
He's presenting his luminous ageing skin…

And you? You're almost facing me,
torso slightly turned away,
bending a little; I can see
the flat line where once they cut
the harmless lump from your right breast
and part of the pectoral muscle's missing,
taking me back to our terror
before the test results, the sunny morning
when three drakes, two grey, one white,
visited our garden in a line, pursuing
the ants with their tiny gabblings.

Three's lucky, that means it'll be benign;
that's how my magical thinking went
as I washed my hands by the window.
And now, as I watch the doctor checking,
your left breast protrudes to a point and,
with your leaning forward, it droops,
more womanly-seeming perhaps,
in this, your ninth decade.

I can see the minute wrinkles
in your folding skin, like the repeating
grooves and grain in the olive trunk
I once drew in pen and ink.
While the doctor's finding nothing
an even deeper tenderness than
I've yet known catches me.

You've had all this life with me
and I see how your skin conveys
your body's history, the drawing
of each breath, how each heartbeat's
measured in creases of flesh.

This

This place, this patch of the valley
has nurtured us for years.

Some days
the trees shake a little
and the river roars,
wanting us
to loosen our foothold.

Hawthorn

'... and other vocalized sorrows of the trees...'

Thomas Hardy, *The Woodlanders*

When I was young I dreamt that the winds would stop:
they were not to come to where I stand
overlooking the sea, on a chalk spur,

not to push in from the south west, day in,
day out, night after night, in the growing season,
worst through the lean months.

With the shove of air against every limb
it would have been easy to lose my grip;
standing up to weather became a way of life;

and with my dreams that the winds would stop
I didn't notice how I was slowly changing;
how the winds were shaping

the pattern of my dance,
stretched towards the north-east
with peculiar grace.

Wall

The brambles are creeping up
from where she cut them down those long,
cold days she laboured to rebuild it

in the hope it might hold back the tides
if they rose in the water meadow,
should there be another flood.

The sand and cement she'd heave to a board
with a hoist and I'd see her mix the mortar,
lift and place each stone; she worked

like the sculptor in clay she'd been,
growing the wall to her will each afternoon,
in unexpected ways, until

the fever took her to her bed and the wall lay still.
The top course steps down to jagged
edges of stone that lurch toward the silent tides.

She always hated the church and, while she was ill,
she told me, she saw the vicar turn
into a bat and fly straight at her face.

The pulley she used hung in the alder,
for months, like a gallows over the wall,
before her husband took it down.

Escape At The Kite Festival
Eggardon Hillfort

Steadily into forget-me-not blue
towards flying pink legs, towards...

Look! A red box with four red tails –
sky swooper, twirler, loop-the-looper –

The child sees a friend, moves,
nearly cuts someone's string.
As I start to wind his in for him,
it slips my grip; strays on a gust,
small blue handle bobbing
across the deep bowl of the next field.

The child runs, runs after
his wind-born climber, crying,

I want my kite, I want my kite...

up grass rampart, down grass ditch,
rampart, ditch, down again, we run.
For a moment, I admire the kite's
break into a separate life...
Then a young man vaults the barbed
wire fence, to search the empty pasture;

before the kite can sail out to sea,
he hauls it from its brave escape,
puts its handle back
into the child's delighted hand
which flies it true now and high,
till all the string's paid out.

16mm...

If time were like a film I'd wind it
backwards and we'd begin again.
We'd join our film, go through our moves
and sing again. Let's be
pure celluloid, just you and me.
We'll keep on dancing...

First Snow

naked trees lean
towards where sun's been,
each limb wearing
its slight white shawl.

Notes

p.21 'Naming Scelidosaurus'
Its fossils have been found exclusively near Charmouth in Dorset and are known for their excellent preservation. Scelidosaurus is the most completely known dinosaur of the British Isles.

p.43 'Visiting Norrie'
Norrie Woodhall, 1905-2011, was the daughter of Augusta Way, a milkmaid thought to be the original inspiration for Tess in *Tess of the d'Urbervilles*. Norrie was probably the last remaining person to have known Thomas Hardy. The New Hardy Players were formed at her request in 2005, on her 100th birthday, and she trod the boards herself.

p.48 'Perseids'
'Meteor' in planet's atmosphere, 'meteoroid' outside it.

Acknowledgements

Poems in this collection have been published in *Stand* and *The Frogmore Papers*.

'The Musicologist And The Birdwatcher', 'Hawthorn', 'Wall' and 'Autumn Song' were published by Happenstance in *Who's In The Next Room*, and performed at King's Place, London; Max Gate, Dorchester and other venues.

'June Notes' was set to music by Peter Hope and performed by Lesley-Jane Rogers at the 3rd William Alwyn Festival, in Southwold Church.

A version of 'Brim' – Summer Sings – was set to music by Peter Hope and premiered by Lesley-Jane Rogers at Manchester University, at a celebration for the 80th birthday of Gordon Crosse.

'Visit', 'Distances ii', 'Distances iii' and 'Perseids' were set to music by David Dubery as 'The Colour of Words', of which 'Visit' was premiered by James Gilchrist in Gloucester Cathedral.

'16mm....', 'A Certain Morning' and 'Distances i, ii, iii, & iv' were shortlisted for the Templar Poetry Pamphlet Award, and were published in *That Sometimes*, a joint pamphlet with Catherine Simmonds.

'Crab Apple' was longlisted for the Rialto RSPB Nature Poetry Competition.

'The Musicologist And The Birdwatcher' was a prize winner in the Troubadour International Poetry Prize.

'About Exile' was published in *Write To Be Counted*, edited by Nicola Jackson, Kathleen Jones and Jacci Bulman.

'Sky Blue' was published by Richmond University Press in *Forty Voices*.

'Cave' won 3rd prize in the Strokestown Poetry Competition.

'Blown Loose' was commended in the Tonbridge Poetry Competition and published in *Room* by Worple Press.

An earlier version of 'A Certain Morning' was broadcast on BBC Radio 3.

'Young Silver Birches After The Storm' was published in *Salisbury Festival Anthology*.

'You're Almost Facing Me' was shortlisted for the Bridport Prize.

My thanks for invaluable feedback from Barry Tempest, Nadine Brummer and especially to Catherine Simmonds, Paul Hyland and Kate Scott who gave me their time when I was putting it all together. Thanks to my grandson, Henry, for adventures together, and huge thanks to Peter for being there.